Inside My Home

Katie Peters

GRL Consultant Diane Craig,
Certified Literacy Specialist

Lerner Publications ◆ Minneapolis

Lerner Publications
An imprint of Lerner Publishing Group, Inc.
241 First Avenue North
Minneapolis, MN 55401 USA

For reading levels and more information, look up this title at www.lernerbooks.com.

Main body text set in Memphis Pro 24/39
Typeface provided by Linotype.

Photo Acknowledgments
The images in this book are used with the permission of: © Marat Musabirov/iStockphoto, p. 3; © jhorrocks/iStockphoto, pp. 4–5; © fizkes/iStockphoto, pp. 6–7, 16 (pepper); © monkeybusinessimages/iStockphoto, pp. 8–9, 14–15, 16 (sofa); © Weekend Images Inc./iStockphoto, pp. 10–11, 16 (toothbrush); © AleksandarNakic/iStockphoto, pp. 12–13.

Front cover: © monkeybusinessimages/iStockphoto

Library of Congress Cataloging-in-Publication Data

Names: Peters, Katie, author.
Title: Inside my home / Katie Peters ; GRL Consultant Diane Craig, Certified Literacy Specialist.
Description: Minneapolis, MN : Lerner Publications, [2023] | Series: My world (Pull ahead readers - nonfiction) | Audience: Ages 4–7 | Audience: Grades K–1 | Summary: "Engage emergent readers with parts of a home. This title features carefully leveled text and full-color photographs. Pairs with the fiction book Our New Neighbors"— Provided by publisher.
Identifiers: LCCN 2022006403 (print) | LCCN 2022006404 (ebook) | ISBN 9781728475974 (library binding) | ISBN 9781728478890 (paperback) | ISBN 9781728483863 (ebook)
Subjects: LCSH: Dwellings—Juvenile literature.
Classification: LCC GT172 .P45 2023 (print) | LCC GT172 (ebook) | DDC 392.3/6—dc23

LC record available at https://lccn.loc.gov/2022006403
LC ebook record available at https://lccn.loc.gov/2022006404

Manufactured in the United States of America
1 – CG – 12/15/22

Table of Contents

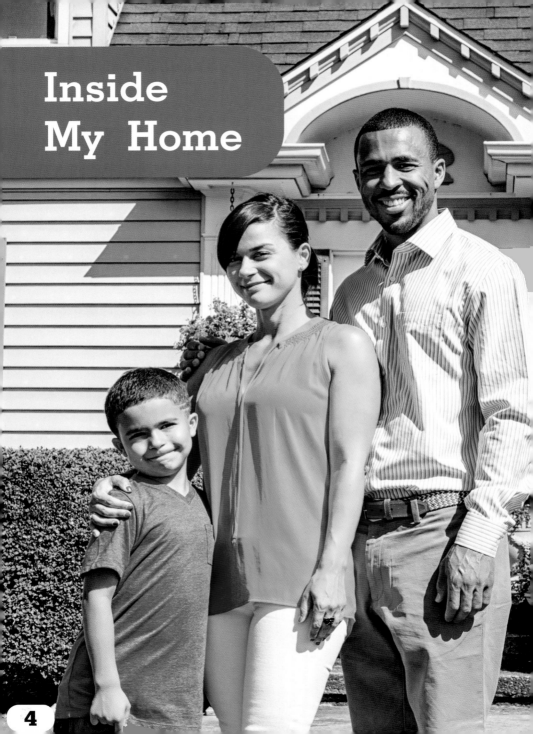

Inside My Home

Everyone needs a home.
I like my home.

This is the kitchen.
I help cook dinner.

This is the living room.
I read on the sofa.

This is the bathroom.
I brush my teeth here.

This is my bedroom.
I share it with my brother.

What is your home like?

What do you like best about your home?

Did You See It?

pepper

sofa

toothbrush

Index